Counting
Earth's
Biomes

Jennifer Kroll

Publishing Credits

Rachelle Cracchiolo, M.S.Ed., *Publisher*
Conni Medina, M.A.Ed., *Managing Editor*
Nika Fabienke, Ed.D., *Series Developer*
June Kikuchi, *Content Director*
Michelle Jovin, M.A., *Assistant Editor*
Lee Aucoin, *Senior Graphic Designer*

TIME For Kids and the TIME For Kids logo are registered trademarks of TIME Inc. Used under license.

Image Credits: All images from iStock and/or Shutterstock.

Library of Congress Cataloging-in-Publication Data

Names: Kroll, Jennifer L., author.
Title: Counting : Earth's biomes / Jennifer Kroll.
Other titles: Earth's biomes
Description: Huntington Beach, CA : Teacher Created Materials, [2017] | Audience: K to grade 3.
Identifiers: LCCN 2017017021 (print) | LCCN 2017020350 (ebook) | ISBN 9781425853426 (eBook) | ISBN 9781425849689 (pbk.)
Subjects: LCSH: Biotic communities--Juvenile literature. | Ecology--Juvenile literature.
Classification: LCC QH541.14 (ebook) | LCC QH541.14 .K76 2017 (print) | DDC 577.8/2--dc23
LC record available at https://lccn.loc.gov/2017017021

Teacher Created Materials

5301 Oceanus Drive
Huntington Beach, CA 92649-1030
http://www.tcmpub.com
ISBN 978-1-4258-4968-9
© 2018 Teacher Created Materials, Inc.
Printed in China
Nordica.082019.CA21901391

Table of Contents

A World of Biomes

A cactus wren nests in a desert cactus. A zebra **grazes** on a grassy plain. A cougar crouches between thick trees in a forest.

Deserts, grasslands, and forests are all biomes.

What Is a Biome?

A biome is a type of area. It has a certain **climate** and look. Earth has land biomes and water biomes. Read along as we count down the five main biomes on Earth.

This cactus wren builds a nest.

This cougar hunts for food.

Home Sweet Habitat

Habitats are found in biomes. Habitats are where plants and animals live. Those plants and animals form **ecosystems**. Some animals help plants. Some plants help animals. Each needs the other to live.

Number 5: Tundras

Biome number five is tundra. Brr! Tundra is a cold climate land biome.

Where on Earth?

Tundras are found near Earth's poles. Parts of Alaska are tundras. Most of Greenland is, too. The tops of some tall mountains are also tundras. Areas of tundra have long winters and cool, short summers.

Tundra Temps

Can you read these thermometers from Greenland? The left one shows how warm it is in summer. The right one shows how cold it is in winter.

summer

winter

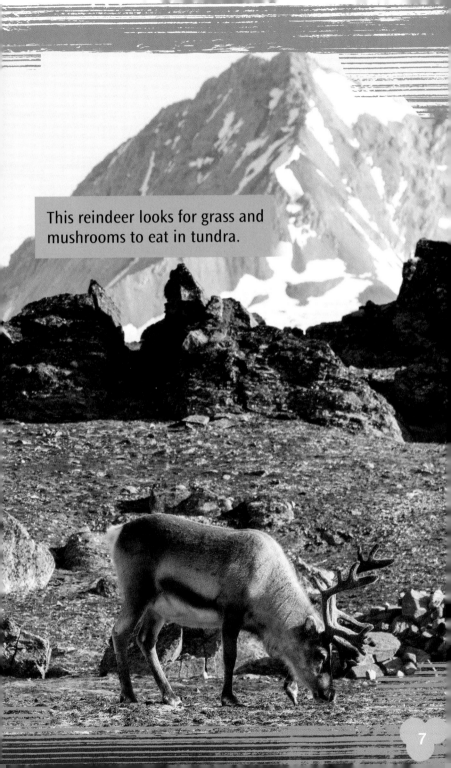

This reindeer looks for grass and mushrooms to eat in tundra.

Tundra Home

It is hard for trees to grow in tundras, but it is still home to many plants and animals. These **species** have **adapted** to the cold.

Wolves roam in some parts of tundra. Foxes and polar bears live there, too. Many birds nest there during the summer.

Freezing Frogs

Wood frogs live in tundras. In winter, the frogs freeze. Their hearts stop. Their blood does not flow. In the spring, they thaw out and hop away!

Polar bears use their layers of fat and fur to stay warm in the freezing tundra.

Number 4: Grasslands

Birds rise out of the tall grass. Prairie flowers bloom. Bison graze.

Welcome to the grasslands. This open space is next on our biome countdown.

Rain on the Plains

Grasslands have a **mild** climate. They are not very wet, but they are not very dry, either. Grasslands can get about 30 inches (75 centimeters) of rain per year.

Huge secretary birds live in grasslands. They are over 4 feet (1 meter) tall!

Land of Many Names

If you are in North America, you will hear grasslands called *prairies*. Head south, and they are called *pampas*. Africans have their own name for grasslands, too. They call them *savannas*.

Bison weigh more than 1,000 pounds (450 kilograms).

Grasslands and People

People use grasslands for farms. They clear out plants. They get rid of insects. These things change the ecosystem.

Natural Grasslands

Some grasslands have not been changed. The Serengeti is in Africa. It is still natural. Lions and zebras call it home.

This Serengeti food pyramid shows what different animals eat.

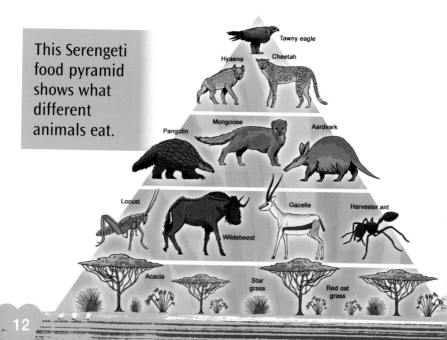

Almost one million zebras live in Serengeti National Park.

Number 3: Deserts

The afternoon sun beats down on the sand. All is quiet. The desert sleeps.

In the evening, the desert biome comes to life. The temperature drops. And animals stir as they awaken.

The Driest Biome

Deserts can be found on all seven **continents**. Deserts are very dry. Some receive less than one inch of rain per year.

This Saharan horned viper stays off of the hot ground by climbing on a plant.

The Liwa desert in Asia is home to some of the most beautiful sand dunes in the world.

Look at the bar graph below. Which biome gets the least rain?

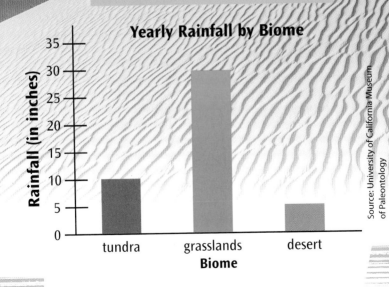

Yearly Rainfall by Biome

Rainfall (in inches)

35
30
25
20
15
10
5
0

tundra   grasslands   desert

Biome

Source: University of California Museum of Paleontology

Water Savers

How do desert plants live in such a dry place? Many are **succulents**. That means they store water in their leaves. Cacti are one type of succulents.

Keeping Cool

Desert animals have tricks for keeping cool. Kangaroo rats stay underground during the day. Ground squirrels use their tails for shade. Lizards switch which foot they stand on to get off the hot sand.

No Water, No Problem

Camels live in the desert. They have adapted to their habitat. They can take water out of the plants they eat. Camels can go up to seven months without stopping to drink.

These cacti collect and store water every time it rains.

Number 2: Forests

Green trees cover the land as far as the eye can see. Forest is next on our biome countdown.

Forests cover a large part of Earth. There are three main types of forests.

Boreal Forest

Boreal forests are found in the cold North. These forests are filled with fir and pine trees. Melting snow supplies the trees with water.

Fir trees like this are common in boreal forests.

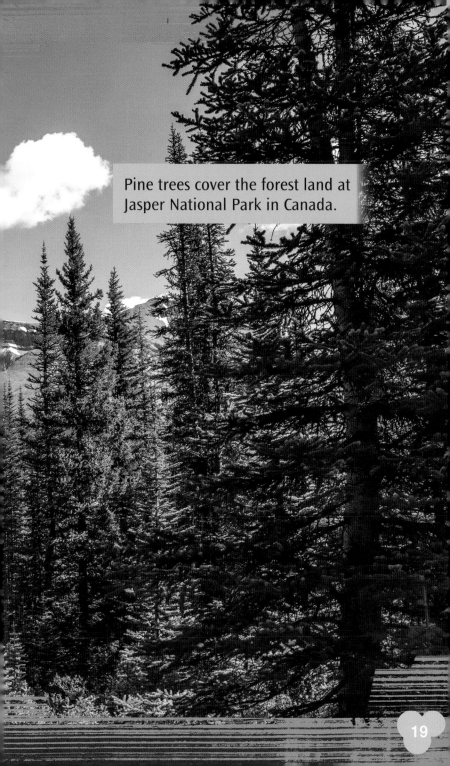

Pine trees cover the forest land at Jasper National Park in Canada.

Temperate Forest

A temperate forest is cold in winter and warm in summer. Temperate forests are full of deciduous (dih-SIJ-yoo-us) trees. These trees lose their leaves in autumn.

Tropical Forests

Tropical forests are home to rain forests. It is warm and wet there. They have many tall trees. These trees do not let in much light. Tropical forests can be dark, even during the day.

The leaves on deciduous trees turn orange and red before falling off.

The leaves from giant trees keep most of the light and heat out of tropical forests.

Full of Life

Rain forests cover only a small part of Earth. But they are home to about half of all plant and animal species.

Number 1: Oceans

Earth's number one biome is the ocean. Water covers most of our planet. That is why the ocean biome tops our countdown.

Water World

Oceans can look quiet from above, but they are full of life. Oceans are home to about two million species of plants and animals. Some live far below the ocean's surface. It is very dark there. Some fish in the deep glow in the dark. Others have lights on their heads to guide their way.

Tang fish can grow up to 20 inches (50 centimeters) long!

Jellyfish use their glow to shock and scare away other animals.

Ocean Ecosystems

Not all parts of the ocean are home to the same species. Some species live near the surface. Others are found near the ocean floor. Each part of the ocean has its own ecosystem.

Coral Reefs

A coral reef is a kind of ocean ecosystem. Corals are small animals. In groups, they climb on rocks. They stay there until they die. Then, more corals climb on top of them. These groups form colorful coral reefs. Reefs are homes to many species.

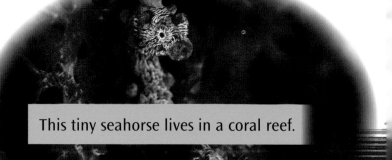

This tiny seahorse lives in a coral reef.

The Great Barrier Reef

The Great Barrier Reef is off the coast of Australia. It is huge! The reef is about the size of 70 million football fields!

At Home in a Biome

There are tundras, grasslands, deserts, forests, and oceans. Each biome is home to many different species. These living things have adapted to life there.

What Is Your Biome?

You live in a biome, too. Go outside and look around. Do you live in a desert? Or maybe you live in grasslands? Could it be a temperate forest? Learn more about the biome you call home.

Toucans live in rain forests.
This toco toucan is easy to
spot by its bright orange beak.

Glossary

adapted—developed features that help one fit in or survive

climate—the usual weather in a place

continents—the seven large land masses on Earth

ecosystems—communities of plants and animals

grazes—eats grass or other plants

mild—not too hot and not too cold

species—certain types of plants or animals

succulents—plants with thick leaves or stems that help them store water